Electricity

John and Janet Clemence

Macdonald

Series Consultant:
David Marshall
Rocks Park School

Technology Consultant:
John Stevenson
Science Museum, London

Editor: Daphne Butler
Designer: Ewing Paddock
Picture Research: Diana Morris
Production: Ken Holt

Illustrators:
Robert Burns 6, 8, 9R, 16, 18, 20, 21, 22
Julia Orsono 9L, 10-11, 12-13, 24-25
Raymond Turvey/Nick Beringer 14-15, 17, 19, 20-21,
26-27

Photographs:
Mansell Collection 7
David Redfern 17
Science Photo Library 16, 18, 24, 25
Zefa 6, 8, 12, 14, 15, 19, 21-22T, 21-22B

A MACDONALD BOOK

First published in Great Britain in 1987 by

Macdonald & Co (Publishers) Ltd
London & Sydney
A BPCC plc Company

ISBN 0 356 13225 0

Printed and bound in Great Britain by
William Clowes Limited, Beccles and London

Macdonald & Co (Publishers) Ltd
Greater London House, Hampstead Road
London NW1 7QX

British Library Cataloguing in Publication Data
Clemence, John
    Electricity.—(My first technology library; 2).
    1. Electricity—Juvenile literature
    I. Title   II. Clemence, Janet III. Series
    537   QC527.2

    ISBN 0-356-13225-0

How to use this book

First, look at the contents page opposite. Read the list to see if it includes the subject you want. The list tells you what each page is about, and you can find the page with information you need.

In the book, some words are darker than the others. These are harder words. Sometimes there is a picture to explain the word. For example, the word **element** appears on page 18 and there is a picture of it on page 18. Other words are explained in the word list on page 31.

On page 28 you will find a technology project. This project suggests ideas and starting points for discovering technology for yourself.

CONTENTS

WHAT IS IT?   6-15
Light in the darkness   6-7
How do you make it?   8-9
How do you get it?   10-11
Electricity at home   12-13
Machines at work   14-15

WAYS WE USE IT   16-27
A bright idea   16-17
Getting hot   18-19
Make a sound   20-21
Many motors   22-23
Computer talk   24-25
Staying safe   26-27

TECHNOLOGY TO TRY   28-30
Making electricity safe   28-30

WORD LIST   31

Light in the darkness

What would life be like without electricity? What would you do when it got dark? There would be no electric light to switch on and no television or radio to cheer you up.

Have you ever used candles during a **power cut**? One candle doesn't give you a lot of light.

Can you imagine a town at night without street lights, car headlamps or brightly lit signs? Electricity is so much part of our lives it is difficult to imagine life without it.

ere was a time when people did not
ow that electricity existed. But slowly
er hundreds of years they began to
derstand it. Many people made
portant discoveries. These discoveries
re like the pieces of a jigsaw; they
eded fitting together. In 1831 Michael
raday did an experiment that was to
nge history. He discovered how to
ke electricity from **magnetism**.

ook some time for the **inventors** to turn
se discoveries into things useful to
ople but by 1900 a few people had
electric light and telephones, and there
was an electric train on the London
Underground. Some well-known people
who lived at this time were Thomas
Edison, Alexander Bell and Guglielmo
Marconi. Perhaps you could find out what
they did and when, and why they are so
famous.

Since 1900 there have been so many
inventions that our lives are now ruled by
all kinds of electrical and **electronic**
machines. We would find it very difficult to
live without them.

How do you make it?

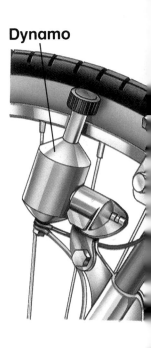

Dynamo

Sometimes your hair flies up when you brush it on a cold day. Some clothes can give you a mild tingling feeling when you undress. **Nylon** shirts may make quite loud crackling sounds. These things happen because you make **static electricity**.

Clouds in a thunderstorm make so much static electricity that you can see it flashing across the sky. Benjamin Franklin caught some of this electricity by flying a kite in a thunderstorm. He was very lucky not to have killed himself. Never try this yourself.

You can make enough electricity for you bicycle lamp by pedalling your bike. You need a tiny **generator** called a **dynamo** fixed to the wheel of your bicycle. As you pedal and the bicycle wheel turns, the magnet in the dynamo turns inside a coil of wire making electricity flow in the wire. The electricity makes the lamp glow. The faster the bicycle wheel turns the brighter the light shines.

Some fruit can be used to make small amounts of electricity. If you push a piece of zinc and a piece of copper into a lemon you turn the lemon into a **battery**. It gives a small amount of electricity that is enough to make an electric clock work.

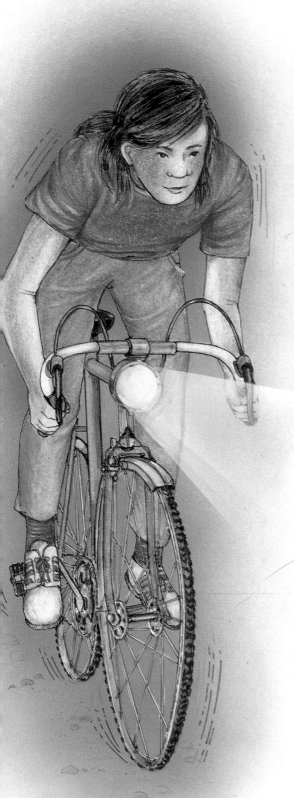

Making static

Rub a balloon on a woollen jumper. Rub it as quickly as you can several times. Now hold the balloon against a wall and let go. What happens to your balloon?

What does this show you?

This clock works with lemons, or grapefruit or even Coca Cola

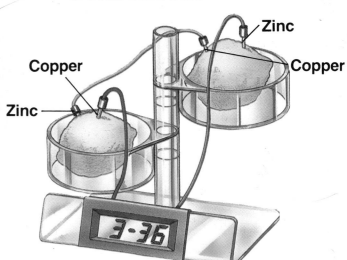

Zinc

Copper

Zinc

Copper

9

How do you get it?

Most of the electricity we use at home is made in a **power station**. Some power stations burn coal or oil. Others use water, **nuclear energy**, or wind.

The electricity travels from the power station along thick wires. These are either buried below the ground so that they cannot be damaged, or they are held high in the air by tall metal towers called **pylons**.

The wires go into your home at the electricity **meter**.

Electricity meter

The whole country is criss-crossed by a network of heavy electricity **cables**. This is called the **national grid**. Because the power stations feed their electricity into the national grid we can all be sure of our supply of electricity even if the power station nearest to us breaks down. If the power station runs out of coal we can still use electricity coming from power stations using a different **fuel**.

The electricity carried by the national grid is very strong. When it reaches a town or village it must be made weaker and shared out between all the houses and factories. This happens at a special place called a **substation**. There may be one near your home.

Pylons

Power station

Electricity substations are
very dangerous places
You should never play near one

Electricity
substation

11

Electricity at home

Fuse box

Ring m

Think about the sitting room or kitchen in your home. How many things are there that use electricity?

How many of them make sounds?
How many of them give light?
How many of them give heat?
How many of them have parts which move?

We use electricity for many things that we don't even think about. We only notice electricity when something goes wrong or there is a **power cut**.

The electricity that comes into your hom from the **national grid** is called **mains** electricity. Great care is taken when the electricity supply is put into a house because mains electricity can kill or seriously injure you. The wires are covered in strong plastic to make them safe. This covering is called **insulation**.

The electricity **cables** in your home are carefully buried in the walls of your hou or fastened below the floor or above the ceiling. Some of the cables go to the lights. They start at the mains **fuse box** near the **meter** and take electricity to ea light hanging from the ceiling. Each ligh has a switch so you can switch the ligh on and off.

...her cables take electricity to each ...ectricity **socket** in the walls. You can ...ug into these sockets for things like the ...evision or the washing machine. The ...bles start from the fuse box, link to each ...cket, and then go back to the meter. ...is is called a **ring main**.

With 1 unit of electricity
With 1 unit of electricity you can cook:

500 pints of soup,
48 meringues,
139 pancakes, or
2½ kg chips.
You can toast 38 sandwiches, or make 71 yoghurts.
You can also polish a floor for 4 hours, or sharpen 15,000 knives.

Machines at work

There are many machines at work in the world. They use electricity to help people in their jobs. Many jobs are hard work. The electric machines make them easier and quicker to do.

Think about building a factory. Electric machines help the builders in all sorts of ways.

A fork lift truck helps move heavy parts from place to place. Tools like electric drills and saws and paint sprayers help make the factory a good place to work in. It would take a long time if there was no electricity.

Paint sprayer

Electricity helps to lift heavy loads

Factories make things like cans of bake beans or vacuum cleaners which are lat sold. They use electrical machinery for kinds of different jobs. Some of the machines need people to work them, bu more and more of the machines are controlled by computers. The people jus check the machines to make sure they working properly. In the offices people organise selling the goods made by the factory and buying the things needed to make more goods. These people have many electrical machines to help them.

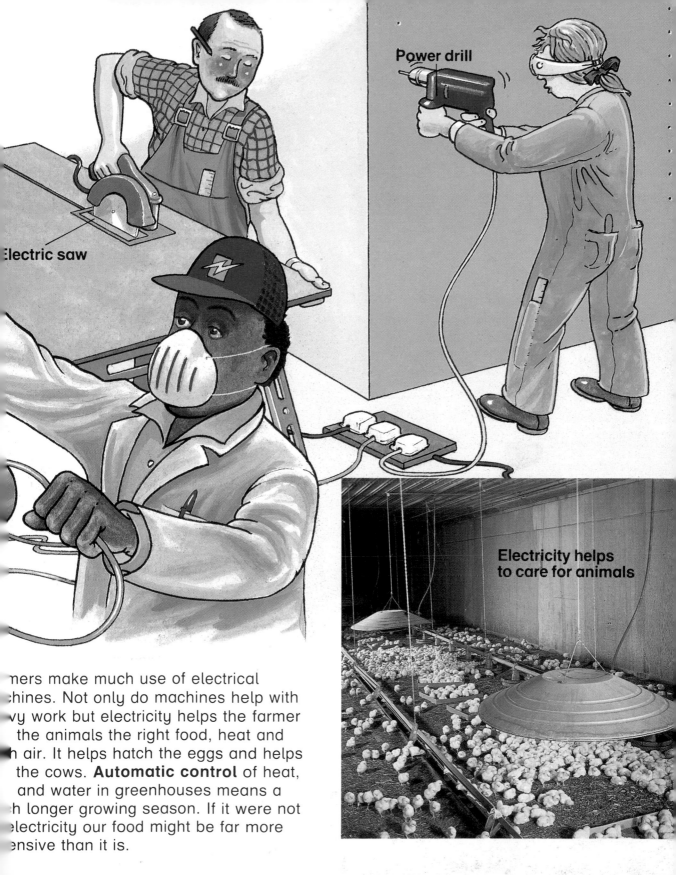

Electric saw

Power drill

Electricity helps
to care for animals

...rmers make much use of electrical
...chines. Not only do machines help with
...vy work but electricity helps the farmer
... the animals the right food, heat and
...h air. It helps hatch the eggs and helps
... the cows. **Automatic control** of heat,
... and water in greenhouses means a
...h longer growing season. If it were not
...electricity our food might be far more
...ensive than it is.

A bright idea

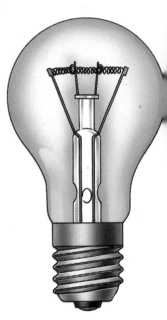

You can switch on the electric light at any time of day or night. People at home, at school, or at work need the light to see what they are doing. Lamps in the streets make them safer for people travelling at night.

Powerful lights help doctors and dentists in their work. Miners have torches built into their helmets. They can see what they are doing under ground but still have their hands free for work.

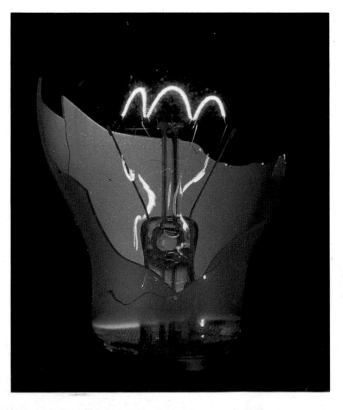

The light bulb is a very common thing in our lives but it took the **inventors** quite time to make one that worked well. The thin wire in modern light bulbs gets whi hot which is why the light is so bright. glass of the bulb is completely **air-tigh** and filled with a special gas which stop the special thin wire from burning away There are now many kinds of electric lamps and **fluorescent** lights which giv out different kinds and amounts of light

DID YOU KNOW?

How much light?

Light bulbs are rated by the amount of electricity they use. In your home you may find light bulbs rated as:

40 watts, 60 watts, 100 watts, or 150 watts.

Which one do you think uses the most electricity? Which one gives out the most light?

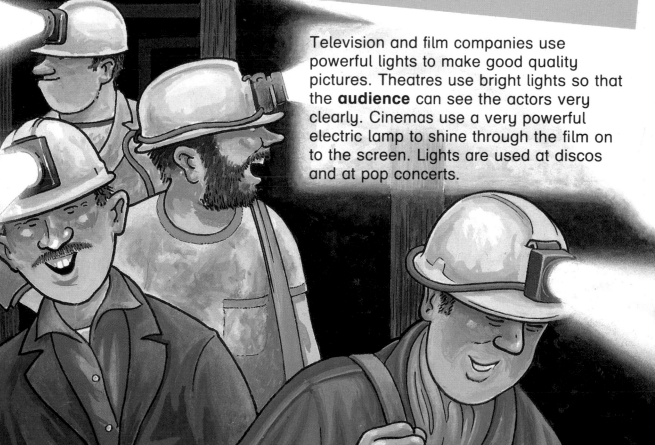

Television and film companies use powerful lights to make good quality pictures. Theatres use bright lights so that the **audience** can see the actors very clearly. Cinemas use a very powerful electric lamp to shine through the film on to the screen. Lights are used at discos and at pop concerts.

Getting hot

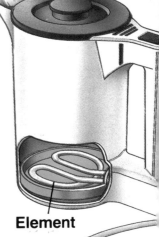

How many things can you think of that use electricity and get hot? Have you ever seen an electric fire? The wire glows brightly when the fire is switched on. When electricity flows through the wire it makes the wire hot. There are also wires like these inside a hair drier and a toaster.

Electricity makes things get very hot. Hot enough to turn clay into bricks, or to melt metals so that they join together, or to cook many things like bread, baked beans or crisps.

Element

Electricity can melt metals

You can heat water very quickly in an electric kettle. The part which gets hot is called the **element**. The element has a covering of **insulation** which keeps the electricity away from the water but lets the heat pass through. This covering makes the kettle safe. There are also elements things like electric irons, hot water tanks and washing machines.

Electricity can bake clay

When you use an iron you need a different heat for different kinds of clothes – hot for cotton but cool for nylon. You choose the right heat by setting the thermostat. A thermostat is a switch which turns off when the temperature gets too high, and on again when the temperature gets too low. The thermostat switches the electricity on and off and keeps the temperature at the right level. Many of the electrical things that we use every day contain a thermostat.

Make a sound

Do you have a door bell for your front door at home? When you press the button a bell rings inside your house. The ringing sound is made by a beater banging against a metal **dome**.

The button is a small switch. When you push the button it switches on the electricity which makes the bell work. When you take your finger off the button the electricity is switched off and the bell stops.

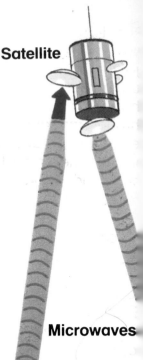

Satellite

Microwaves

You can call a friend at any time .

Electric door bell

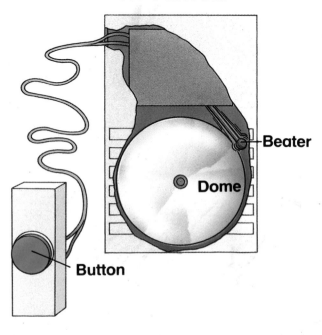

Beater

Dome

Button

People use electricity in more complicated ways to make sound. When you talk to your friend on the telephone your voice is turned into electricity by a **microphone** in the **mouthpiece**. The electricity travels through the telephone wire to your friend's telephone. Your friend hears your voice because the electricity is turned back into sound by a **loudspeaker** in the **earpiece**.

We can talk to people on the other side of the world because electrical signals can be turned into **microwaves** and bounced off **satellites** high above the Earth. The microwaves are then turned back into electricity and then back into sound.

People make use of microphones and loudspeakers in radios, record players and tape recorders and in many electrical machines.

Inside a telephone

Loudspeaker

Microphone

. . . even when your friend lives on the other side of the world

Many motors

An electric motor makes things move. Many machines have an electric motor and that is why they turn or twist, or suck or blow, or move in any way at all.

Think about a food mixer. The motor makes the beaters turn round and mix the food. Look at an electric fan. The motor makes the fan spin round and makes the air move like a wind.

Can you think of any other machines which have an electric motor?

What happens when you switch on the motor?

TRY THIS

Making an electromagnet

Wrap some thin insulated wire around a large nail about 30 times. Strip the covering from each end of the wire. Connect the bare ends of the wire to a 3 volt battery. Your nail will now be an electromagnet and should pick up pins and paperclips.

Trains and trolley buses have big powerful electric motors. The electricity is carried by wires overhead or by a rail alongside the track. The motor uses the electricity to drive the wheels.

People would very much like to make an electric car. It would be very quiet and there would be no smelly fumes. But a car would need **batteries** to give the electricity. It would be too dangerous and complicated to have cars attached to wires or rails by the roads. People cannot make a battery that is small enough, light enough and powerful enough for the car to go fast and to travel hundreds of miles. There are some electric trucks used for short slow journeys or moving baggage round a station. Their batteries are charged up at night from the **mains**.

Computer talk

Do you have a computer at school? It probably sits on a trolley and shares a corner of your classroom. You may have one at home as well. What do you do with the computer?

Not many years ago a computer cost a lot of money and each computer needed a whole room to itself. Only a few people ever used a computer. Now there are lots of computers in all sorts of places. The computers are much easier to use, and many people use them every day. They have changed people's lives in lots of ways.

The computer centre

A computer in a classroom can be used i many ways because you can put differen programs into its memory. You can ask the computer questions and it can give you answers so it can be used to help yo learn. You can use the computer to write stories, and if you make mistakes you ca correct them very easily. When your stor is finished you can print it out on a printe

You can control a **floor turtle** or **robot arm**. You can draw pictures perhaps with the help of a **mouse**. The computer migh connect to the telephone line through a **modem** so that messages can be sent to other computers. Then you can talk to other computers anywhere in the world.

How do you use the computer in your school?

A silicon chip

...hings like computers, but also televisions ...nd radios, use special electrical **circuits** ...lled **electronic** circuits. Often today ...ngineers talk about micro-electronics ...ecause the circuits are now so tiny that ...ey fit on to a small piece of **silicon** ...lled a chip. Micro-electronics has made ...anges in all our lives. Not only have ...mputers appeared in many classrooms ...t also in offices, shops, banks, factories ...d even living rooms.

25

Staying safe

Electricity is very useful, clean and powerful, but it is also dangerous. **Mains** electricity is so powerful that it can kill you.

You have to take great care that you do not touch bare wires carrying mains electricity. If you do you will get an electric shock.

There are warning signs which tell us about dangerous electrical machinery. You will see them near to electricity substations, railway tracks, and electricity pylons. Always obey them.

Whenever we use electricity it is important to put safety first. Wires should never be left trailing across the floor where people can tread on them or trip over them. Or even worse, animals should not be allowed to chew wires. Wires should be checked regularly to make sure that the **insulation** is not damaged.

If you are asked to pull a plug out of a **socket** you should make sure that your hands are not wet, then switch the socket off, if it has a switch. When you pull the plug out you should hold it by its plastic or rubber body. Never put your fingers near the pins. Never poke anything into an electric socket, or into any electrical machine which is plugged into the **mains**. It is very dangerous.

When wires become too hot they can start a fire. To stop this happening every house has a **fuse box**. A fuse is a special piece of wire which melts if too much electricity flows through it. When the wire melts the electricity can no longer flow and is turned off. Sometimes the mains has special switches called circuit breakers instead of fuses. Circuit breakers switch themselves off if too much electricity flows through them. You will find a box near to the **meter** in your house. It will contain either fuses or circuit breakers for all the mains electricity in your house.

27

Making electricity safe

BEGIN HERE

The biggest problem with electricity is that it is very, very dangerous and needs treating with care to keep it safe. Some things, like metals, let electricity pass through them. These are called conductors. Other things won't let electricity pass through them at all. These are called insulators. You are going to find out about how we make electricity safe.

First of all, look at these two pages. Try reading **Look around** and the story about Mrs Sparks. On page 30 there are some investigations for you to try. Finding out about something is called research. You are doing research into making electricity safe. Try to make notes about your research while you are doing it. It helps you remember later.

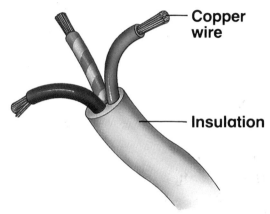

Copper wire

Insulation

Mrs Sparks

The school was having a talk abou electricity. Mrs Sparks was coming from the local science museum. Class 3W were very excited as the jostled each other down the corrido and into the hall. It was a good five minutes before everyone sat down and stopped chattering. Mrs Spark stood up and started to speak.

"Electricity is a bit like you childre It runs all over the place and can get out of hand if we're not careful Each bit of electricity is carried by something called an electron. Imagine that all of you are

Look around

Whenever you are out and about look round for electricity. Look out for pylons and cables, for neon signs, telephone wires, electric trains. When you go to the shops look for those selling electrical goods. Look at all the plugs and sockets and switches, all the different kinds of light bulb, all the different kinds of wire.

Get a grown up to give you some spare bits of electric cable and a spare plug. These must not be joined to the mains.

Examine the plug carefully. Undo the screws with a screwdriver and look inside. What parts do you think the electricity passes through? What are these made of? What parts keep the electricity safe? What are these made of?

Look at the cable. How many wires are there inside? Can you find out what each one does? Where does the electricity pass through? Which bits keep the electricity safe?

Places

Your local power station
Your local electricity or DIY shop
A museum such as:
The Milne Electricity Museum, Tonbridge, Kent
The Science Museum, London
The Engineerium, Brighton, East Sussex

Books

Children's Britannica *under* Electricity.
Electricity, Julie Fitzpatrick, Electricity Council, 1986.
Electricity in and around the home, Anthony Byers, Electricity Council, 1986.
Electric Power, Ed Catherall, Wayland, 1981.

Words

You will come across some unusual words in your investigations. If you do not know the meaning of a word you could try the word list on page 31 of this book, or better still use a dictionary. Here are some of the words you may need to look up:

circuit	conductor
current	insulator
electrician	volt

electrons. What happens at breaktime? The bell goes, you all jump up, and push and shove your way down the corridor to the playground. But you have to go down the corridor, don't you? You can't go through the walls."

Here Mrs Sparks paused and waved a bit of electric cable in the air.

"Electrons are just the same as you. Can you see these shiny copper bits in the cable? Those are like the corridor, and these grey plastic bits round the outside, those are like the walls. Things that let electrons through, like the wire, are called conductors, and things that keep electrons out, like the plastic, are called the insulators.

You can test things to see whether they are insulators or conductors. But first you must make your equipment.

Insulator tester

Take three pieces of wire about 15 centimetres long and firmly fix crocodile clips to each end. Screw the bulb holder to a piece of wood. Now connect them all together with a battery to make a circuit. Does the bulb light up?

Screw two metal cup hooks into another piece of wood. Put them about 5 centimetres apart. Now add this to your circuit.

Collect some materials

You need to collect some test materials. They need to be more than 5 centimetres long so that they fit between the cup hooks. Try:

paper	floor tile
card	wood
key	rubber tube
bare wire	crayon
plastic	ball point pen

Testing

Press each test piece down very firmly on to the cup hooks. If the bulb lights it is a conductor. If it does not light it is an insulator. Record your results.

Bulb lights up	Bulb doesn't light up

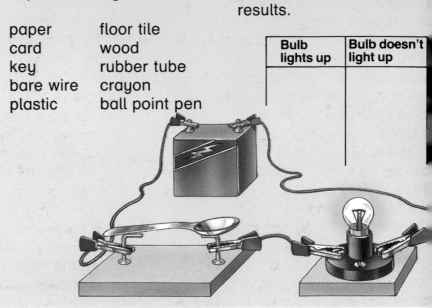

TAKE IT FROM HERE

You have found out about insulators and conductors. You have looked at electricity in the world around you. You could make your own book called *Making electricity safe.*

Perhaps you can find poems and stories about electricity. Can you make up a piece of music which sounds like an electric machine. You could try to make a model which uses a battery to make it work.

Things you need

For insulator tester

a collection of different things	
4.5 volt battery	6 crocodile clips
3 volt bulb	2 cup hooks
bulb holder	2 pieces of wood
3 pieces of wire	screwdriver

Things to test

a collection of different things